LET IT HATCH

Let the life live

DUSHYANT DAS

INDIA • SINGAPORE • MALAYSIA

ISBN 979-8-89363-347-4

Dedicated to

"baba"

My father never taught me life because he himself was a wonderful manifestation of life.

Just seeing him was learning life.

Just talking to him was learning life.

Just touching him was touching life.

Just listening to him was listening to life.

His smile was the most beautiful depiction of grief and pain.

The way he handled disrespect and deceit was fathomless.

The way he respected everyone, even those who thought him to be nothing was lovable.

The way he created the aura of abundance around all the scarcities we faced during our childhood was awesome.

The way he entitled his kids us with all the freedom for life is rare.

His non-interference in his kids' life made each one of them capable of getting educated profoundly.

The man who trusted people beyond the scales of trust irrespective of what they rendered him back.

The way he nurtured his kids, cared for his mother, obeyed his father and cared for his wife is The God's Way.

The son of a rich zamindar

A poor farmer

&

The simplest human being.

✳ ✳ ✳

Why this book?

Title: "Let It Hatch: Navigating Through the Speed and Rigour of Modern Living"

In the hustle and bustle of our lives, there comes a book that transcends the ordinary, a book that is not just another addition to your collection, but a guide for your journey - "Let It Hatch." Each word within these pages carries the weight of personal experience, a chronicle of the author's own trials and triumphs.

As the author opens the chapters of their life, the urgency to share their insights becomes apparent. The clock is ticking, and the message is clear - the time to reflect and understand is now. "No one knows how much time is available. So, the sooner the better." These words echo the essence of a book written with a sense of immediacy, urging readers to delve into its pages without delay.

A unique facet of "Let It Hatch" lies in its universality. Every page is a mirror reflecting the shared experiences of the author and, by extension, every reader. It is a profound exploration of the common threads that weave through the tapestry of our lives. The author, a teacher intimately connected to the youth, recognizes the impatience and lack of perseverance prevalent in today's fast-paced world.

In a society where relationships and friendships are often strained, "Let It Hatch" stands as a beacon of understanding. The author acknowledges the struggles people face in navigating these intricate human connections. "People are suffering because of relationships and friendships," a poignant observation that sets the stage for a discourse on finding solace and understanding in the midst of societal complexities.

The metaphorical speed of life has surpassed even the swiftness of light, and the hardness of relations has rivalled that of diamonds. The author, however, does not merely point out these challenges; they extend a hand to guide readers through the turbulence. This book is an offering of wisdom gained through a lifetime of experiences, an attempt to make sense of the chaos and to provide a compass for those seeking direction.

"My effort is to share my experiences and learnings from my own life. To make it more generic than specific, is my goal." These words encapsulate the author's mission - to distil personal experiences into universal lessons, ensuring that every reader finds resonance within these pages.

"Let It Hatch" is not just a book; it is a companion for your life's journey, a source of inspiration and guidance. As you flip through its pages, you may find not just the author's story but fragments of your own, intertwined with the collective human experience.

God Bless.

✹ ✹ ✹

"In the Uncharted Territory of Friendship: A Serendipitous Journey"

In the vast landscape of life, the concept of friendship defies the rules of search, selection, and predictability." You can't search, you can't select & you can't find a friend of your likes." These words resonate with the elusive nature of true companionship, emphasizing that genuine friendships are not products of deliberate choices but rather serendipitous gifts.

The emergence of friends is a phenomenon intricately woven with the fabric of time and circumstance. Friendships unfold, revealing their true colors over days, months, or even an entire lifetime. The timeline is but a secondary factor; what truly defines a friend goes beyond the limitations of a clock or calendar.

The duration of interactions and the time spent together are not the measuring sticks for the authenticity of a friendship. Unlike in other aspects of life, where time can be a decisive factor, friendships defy such constraints. A friend might walk into your life for a brief moment, yet the impact can be profound and everlasting.

Friends have a unique ability to appear seemingly out of nowhere, like unexpected stars lighting up the night sky. It is this unpredictability that adds an element of magic to the journey of companionship. They imprint on our lives in ways that are often indescribable, leaving an enduring mark on our hearts and souls.

The essence of true friendship lies in its spontaneity and genuine connection, transcending the boundaries set by time and conventional expectations. A friend is not someone you choose based on specific criteria; rather, they become an integral part of your life through shared experiences, mutual understanding, and an unspoken bond.

As we navigate the uncharted territory of friendship, let us embrace the beauty of these unexpected connections. True friends may not be found through a deliberate search or selection process, but their presence enriches our lives in ways that surpass our wildest expectations. In the end, it's not about the time it took to call someone a friend; it's about the depth of the connection and the impact they have on our journey through life.

✳ ✳ ✳

"Navigating the Tides of Change in Friendship: A Call for Patience and Vigilance"

In the ever-shifting landscape of life, the axiom "Change is the only constant" echoes loudly, particularly within the realm of friendships. The dynamics between friends can evolve, sometimes in unexpected and challenging ways. How we respond to these changes is a delicate balance that requires patience, understanding, and a keen sense of observation.

The advice resonates: "Never react to the changes you observe in your friend until and unless you are sure that he or she would give it a heed." It emphasizes the importance of restraint and a thoughtful approach when witnessing transformations in a friend's behaviour or circumstances. Jumping to conclusions prematurely may not serve the friendship well.

As a friend, the responsibility extends beyond mere observation. It involves being a critic, providing constructive feedback when necessary. However, the author acknowledges the potential for mental retaliation that may arise from such well-intentioned critiques. Friendship, after all, is a delicate balance between honesty and tact.

Change, the author asserts, is not only inevitable but often necessary. It can be a response to circumstantial or behavioural factors, and while it may be challenging to witness, it is a natural part of the human experience. The threshold of patience and tolerance is crucial; until the changes start causing harm beyond acceptable limits, a degree of acceptance is advocated.

The narrative takes a poignant turn when describing the pain associated with seeing a friend drift away into an undesirable path. The author encourages a role of observation, urging friends to be vigilant without judgment. The metaphorical darkness signifies the potential pitfalls that a friend may encounter, and it becomes the responsibility of the observer to be ready to intervene before the journey becomes irreversibly bleak.

The guiding principle is one of balance. Be good and patient, but not to the extent of losing one's natural being. The call is to remain neutral and calm, waiting for the ebb and flow of time to present an opportunity to be the friend's saviour against the undesirable change.

In essence, the narrative encourages a nuanced and patient approach to evolving friendships. It recognizes the inevitability of change while emphasizing the importance of being a steadfast and observant friend, ready to navigate the tides of transformation and provide support when needed most.

"Embracing the Wisdom of Priorities: A Journey from Illusions to Peace"

In the fleeting tapestry of life, the profound truth emerges: "Life is actually too short to be spent on and spent with people for whom you are an option and not a priority." The narrative unfolds with a candid reflection on the author's experiences, navigating the complex terrain of friendships that turned out to be ephemeral illusions.

The author candidly shares the realization that not all friends are steadfast companions in both joy and sorrow.

Having invested time and energy in proclaiming these friendships to the world, the author discovered the hollowness when adversity struck. Friends who were seemingly present during moments of pleasure swiftly transformed, their priorities shifting from shared experiences to a focus solely on their individual pursuits.

The author's revelation, both poignant and eye-opening, unveils a painful truth – the supposed friendship was not built on genuine connection but rather on the material wealth that the author possessed. It was a sobering realization that prompted a re-evaluation of relationships and priorities.

Fortunately, life bestowed invaluable teachers and parents upon the author, imparting the wisdom of immaterialism. The upbringing instilled a profound understanding of the importance of genuine connections, empathy, and shared experiences over material possessions. It served as a lifeline during the challenging period of recognizing and disentangling from superficial friendships.

The journey towards detachment and self-discovery was undoubtedly difficult, marked by moments of solitude and introspection. However, the author emerged from the chaos with a newfound peace. The mantra became clear: "If I am a 'nothing' for them, then I am nothing for their life too." The acceptance of this reality paved the way for a serene detachment from toxic relationships.

The narrative closes with a poignant message of encouragement, extending a hand to those who may find themselves entangled in similar webs. The author, having navigated the storm with grace and resilience, offers assurance that one can emerge from such situations peacefully and without carrying the burden of expectations.

In essence, the story is a testament to the transformative power of self-realization and the wisdom gained through life's trials. It encourages readers to embrace the lesson that life is too short to be spent on relationships devoid of authenticity, urging them to find solace in detachment and the pursuit of meaningful connections.

✳ ✳ ✳

"The Delicate Art of Letting Go: Knowing When to Bid Adieu"

In the intricate tapestry of friendships, the truth stands stark: "No friend is forever." The narrative embarks on a journey exploring the profound and sometimes painful realization that friendships, like seasons, undergo transformations. Central to this exploration is the delicate art of leaving when a friend's evolution takes a toll on one's well-being.

The author imparts a valuable lesson on confronting change within friendships, especially when it manifests in ways that inflict emotional pain. The approach advocated is one of earnest communication, an endeavour where heartfelt efforts are invested to rectify the friendship's course. The narrative encourages giving numerous chances, tirelessly attempting to bridge the gap created by evolving differences.

However, there comes a point where persistence yields no positive outcome. The author imparts a crucial piece of wisdom: "If, still, things go in vain. Just leave." The phrase encapsulates the essence of recognizing one's boundaries and understanding that self-preservation sometimes necessitates walking away from relationships that no longer serve a positive purpose.

"The art of leaving" is portrayed as a skilful act, an art form that requires courage, introspection, and a commitment to one's own well-being. The narrative refrains from presenting leaving as a defeat but rather as a mindful decision to safeguard one's mental and emotional health. It's an acknowledgment that, in certain instances, departing is an act of self-love and self-respect.

The story subtly challenges the notion that leaving is synonymous with failure, presenting it instead as an empowering choice when confronted with irreparable differences. The art lies not just in the departure but in the wisdom to discern when staying would be a disservice to oneself.

In essence, "The Delicate Art of Letting Go" offers a thoughtful perspective on the impermanence of friendships and the importance of recognizing when to gracefully exit. It provides solace to those grappling with the difficult decision of leaving a friend behind, reminding them that it can be an act of strength, resilience, and ultimately, a form of self-preservation. To my experience, leaving is very important at some stages. Leaving makes the space clear. The space between two friends. This space is the elixir of life.

It mends and repairs everything. Leaving is painful but it's the medicine.

Always remember, in a perfume shop, even if you don't buy, you come out with fragrances.

✻ ✻ ✻

Be the part of a respectful circle.

With time, we grow and our kids too. They should and must have a complete idea about our friends. So, to keep our kids in a respectful circle of theirs, we should first create a respectful circle of our own.

Behaviour and thought process don't need any medium to travel. The more unrest we have in our circle, the more it will get communicated to people around us. Respectfulness is good to be communicated.

So, surround yourself with people who smile when they see you, people whose eyes light up when they see you.

Surround yourself with people who appreciate you for what you are and don't draft you to what they want you to be.

Build a circle of friends which survives and values only respect.

* * *

Be nothing when you are treated like nothing....

You might experience this in some or the other phase of your life. Not just friends but anybody around your fraternity.

Sometimes, our circle treats us like we are nothing. Like we don't even exist. Usually, we respond to such situations instantaneously and also we begin to "judge" people around in that circle.

The blunder following this act is usually talking about it to other people.

This weakens us.

This shows that the people who are treating you like this are right.

And we land up being in more of a chaos than lesser.

Just being silent and non-responsive is the key. Yes, some of my mentors did suggest to me to take a chance by asking them about their behaviour or your feelings but I thought it's ok if they are just one or two of them but still, disrespect in any form is unacceptable.

If they treat you like a 'nothing', then become one for them.

* * *

The best way to end something is to let it starve.

Never water a dead plant.

No action, no response, no discussions, no feeding.

Words always have lesser power than actions. Act and it will be done.

The more you speak on this, the weaker you become because this will make your critics win over you.

Hence, be the power. The powerful have everything that's needed to be silent. Silence is strength.

It will also help you shed your ego.

Not a bad deal, at all.

✳ ✳ ✳

Hurt your friend with the truth.

Never flatter them with lies.

You have all the right to lose one because you spoke the truth but never be afraid of the fear of losing one because of this truth.

You are the one who should be truthful from your side unconditionally.

If you refrain from truth.

You are going to punish yourself and your friend.

Truth is the only nutrition for friendship.

* * *

With whom you can be alone but without loneliness.

A friend makes you one with the self. You must not feel the duality. There doesn't exist the 'other'. Friendship is all about being there with selfless self.

No principal amount, no interest but lifelong fathomless dividends of smiles and peace.

Friendship is love without boundaries of thoughts and without conditions of life.

No society ever accepts friendship because the society is only meant for self-defined tolerance to love and respectfulness.

* * *

He is my friend.

Such an easy statement to deliver.

If you are a friend. It's a responsibility.

If you are a friend then your friend must know that there is someone who won't let me cry.

And the friend would always know that you are always there to stand with him.

Regardless of the perspective, a friend is a friend of yours.

Without any prejudice or judgement.

* * *

Be unburdened...

Friends go out of their way to help a friend. This is a rare act but a really beautiful one.

That's great. Well done!

But if you start feeling betrayed then you have lost it all.

This happens when you start expecting the same.

Expecting is ok.

But if you expect because you did so much then you are intoxicating your own head with the burden of your pure hearted deeds you did.

This creates a pressure on your friend when you expect, in turn.

* * *

Never beg for a friendship.

You can never get a friend with agreements.

The friend you want will arrive when you are ready.

Keep moving with clear and pure intentions.

If you seek, and if you don't receive the same efforts.

Cut them off.

***

When your friend is struggling...

When your friend is crying...

When your friend is lonely...

When your friend is disheartened...

Just say, "Go Onn..."

&

I am here with you in all the mud you are in.

✳ ✳ ✳

You are getting matured.

If you don't get disappointed on small things, you learn to ignore.

If you forgive and move on.

If You cut off from negative people.

If you don't want anything from anybody and you know you get what nature feels you deserve.

If you believe that the almighty is doing the best for you.

These principles are the parameters of a matured friend.

* * *

Excess of agreements is deadly...

If you say "yes" to everything that your friend does then very soon the friend will start taking you for granted and will start doing things that aren't acceptable too.

So, never worry about what the response would be, say "no" if you think what your friend is doing is wrong.

Friendship has to have both criticism and altercations. If you can't rectify your friend, If you fail to show the mirror, you're not a friend.

***

If they didn't, then you do...

If they don't trust you, trust yourself...

If they don't love you, love yourself...

If they don't care for you, care for yourself...

If they aren't there for you

Be there for yourself.

✳ ✳ ✳

If even a single person trusts you blindly, it's priceless.

That person is priceless.

That friendship is priceless.

That person can speak rough to me but will never think bad for me

If you feel you are sure of the fact that the entire world can betray me but 'him'

That's all priceless...

That's trust....

* * *

A true friend accepts you for who you are, and not for what you have and how you are.

They always have time to talk to you irrespective of the last call you made.

They always exist simultaneously with your bad times and take you out of that.

They are those wonderful creatures you can't afford to lose.

So, if you have such a being in your life, stay blessed.

Value them.

* * *

In spite of being very good, you can't always be good.

Because somewhere you will be made 'bad'

And some where you will be proved 'bad'

Let it be.

Don't stop being good.

Don't care about being judged.

***

Always remain indebted.

For any friend who was with you in your bad times.

Just be like 'Karna', he always knew the end result but he was indebted.

Be loyal and indebted to such beautiful friends.

At any cost...

* * *

Be there for your overthinking friends...

Over-thinking friends need over clarifying friends.

Go ahead to render them that clarification they need, if at all you care for the bond you have with them.

Win their trust.

Your actual attitude towards them should only be over loving.

* * *

Be there for a betrayed friend...

Betrayed friends find it very difficult to trust anyone anymore.

They wonder with a fake smile over their face.

They fail to overcome the after effects of the betrayal.

Try with your whole heart and keep trying.

It's difficult for the betrayed to trust even the right person with the right intention.

* * *

Distance & Silence

The best reply to any disrespect in any relationship or friendship are

distance and silence.

Distance will protect you from negative emotions and silence will strengthen you to become positive by retrospection.

Distance and Silence are two extremely strong weapons, not only to win over your sorrows but also to win over your own self.

The Sound of silence enlightens the soul.

Distance lightens the burden.

***

Friends come back.

When they will realize your absence in their life.

When they will get disappointed by others.

When they miss the selfless and reasonless smiles, they shared with you.

When they find themselves in dearth of lighter moments.

When they miss people without intuitions for them, which you had.

When they see that people around them value them for, not what they are but who they are.

When they will not find anyone to disagree with them.

When they will not have friends who feel happy for their happiness.

* * *

Never bother for...

What people think and say about your friend.

Thieves attack homes with something valuable.

Only trees bearing fruits go through stone pelting.

No one bothers aboutr people without value.

Know your friend and nothing is more important than the fact that 'you' know your friend.

Feel proud and be happy that you have a friend whom people don't want you to have.

* * *

Friends change...

> When they hurt enough that they have to.

> When they see enough that they inspire to.

> When they learn enough that they want to.

> When they receive enough that they are able to.

* * *

Speak…

What your friends need to hear and not what they want to hear.

Also, keep it absolutely ruthless and real.

Don't care for the response.

Be the friend who doesn't hit across the bushes but hits you straight at the face.

They might hate you for a short time but later they will love you for the long time.

Until they realize that your words and statements were only for the best of your life.

If you want to kill a friend, make him listen to what he needs to hear.

He is dead, ideally.

* * *

"kupath niwaar, supath chalaawa"

Bring your friend out of the mud of negativities and difficulties. Being a friend is a huge responsibility. Not just sharing and caring but something far bigger than this.

It's your right as well as a duty to tell the truth to your friend. Tell it without any fear of losing the friend. The friend, sooner or later, will not only listen but also understand and realize your point of view as the right way out.

Never let your friend fall into any deep shit. If at all that happens, you have proved to be useless.

✳ ✳ ✳

In a close friendship.

    Choose to ignore the bad

    Deal with the bad with a soft heart

    Focus on all that's good

    Bow down for peace

    Talk less, listen more

    More heart, Lesser brain

✳ ✳ ✳

Never...

Control your friend's decision, support it if possible.

Involve yourself in your friend's relationships, just be curious enough to know

Help your friend after knowing the fact from others that your friend needs your help but help when actually needed.

✻ ✻ ✻

Super skilled friends...

They are always there for a talk, any time, under any situation.

They have the super skill and power to convince our parents for something which we fail to do.

Their counsel is always more valuable for our family members than our own words.

They always know that something is going on in our life.

And they look into our eyes and ask, "kya chal raha hai? bol..."

Such super friends are blessings in disguise.

Never let them go...

***

The guitar with just one string

In a friend circle, there exists a being who speaks only about their own achievements and expertise. These species are usually time killers in boredom. They are harmless to the extent you are in a normal mood.

They are also the crowd puller, when they arrive, the entire circle joins the entertainment. Always keep such species intact in the circle because they have the power to both unburden and enlighten the entire circle with their single string guitar.

And also, these species have a clean and sound reach to everyone else's homes as well. They are the bunch of smiles and they are the ones who will come up late to your help but will dedicate themselves to whatever they can do to support you.

✳ ✳ ✳

Never encroach...

The inner space of a friend.

The space that we all possess and share with either ourselves or with nature.

This space is the most pious and soulful area of our existence. This space is only for our own repairing and refurbishing. This space has the power to rewrite the bad pages of life with a better script and screenplay.

If encroached, you will hate the encroacher.

So, leave that space.

Just keep your distance from this space of your friend.

* * *

People treat you the way they feel about you

What we speak might differ from what we feel because everything can't be expressed. What we convey might not convey what we actually wanted to.

But we always treat someone the way we feel about them. Anything else is always fictitious and not self-pleasing.

And the same is for all. We are treated as we make them feel about us.

* * *

Move on before the defence system gets activated.

Communicate to a friend about their mistakes and move on.

Keep telling them the truth about their wrong doings only to the extent they don't come up with a defence.

Never hold.

And also, be as lighter as possible.

Always mention that 'I think' it should have been like that.

Give them time to reflect and rectify themselves in their inner space.

✳ ✳ ✳

Avoid dysfunctional friends

the more you surround yourself with dysfunctional people, the more dysfunctional you become.

Friends aren't just for talks, walks and gossips.

Friends aren't just for partying and boozing around.

They are for the right functionality of life, our life.

So, be with the functional ones.

* * *

Hurt the right way.

Never hurt your friend with a lie.

The truth may be harsh but exists.

A lie doesn't even exist.

A lie hurts with no possibility of rectifications but the truth, sooner or later makes one reflect on the truth.

So, hurt your friend with the truth.

* * *

The important 'nothing'

  A call for 'nothing'

  A drive for 'nothing'

  A laughter for 'nothing'

  A feast for 'nothing'

  A hangout for 'nothing'

✳ ✳ ✳

If you have these..

People who give importance to your intentions and not your intelligence.

People who don't have any criteria to judge you under any situation.

People who don't measure you on the scales of right and wrong.

Hold them and feel lucky to have these people.

* * *

Not for wins and losses

Friends don't come for our wins and losses.

They just come to walk with us for a mile or two with us.

They come to keep our love alive.

They come to just make us feel our own love for ourselves.

They come to put us into the light.

They come to show us the right path to a reasonless smile.

* * *

Give it a proper closure

It usually happens that we love to tell people about all the bad experiences in friendship and relationships. But I think that if we do, it's gone from our side too.

Never tell people about such experiences.

Reason being the fact that it will not render anything positive and people will get to know about this and they will get an issue to gossip on.

Friendship is absolutely personal. If you are happy or unhappy with someone, never let the world know this. Never.

Give it a proper closure because that which is out of your hands must be out of your mind too.

* * *

Choose the right way

We all have the option to be either an encouragement or a critic.

Critics mushroom around us naturally and are in abundance but there is a huge dearth of encouragers.

Be the one.

***

Don't let your friend know

That you are hurt by his actions or words.

There should always be some moisture of feelings in a friendship.

The drier the sand, the faster it flows out of hands, no matter how strongly you hold it.

＊ ＊ ＊

Purity is not always digestible

Some people will lose you because they don't have any idea about holding and possessing gems with purity.

Let them live with all that's material and artificial.

Just move away into happiness.

✻ ✻ ✻

Both in One...

Every friend is a package of two. A friend and an enemy.

He keeps all your secrets,

He feels jealous when you do something better. That's natural.

And never deny that.

But jealousy should always be within the limits of obsession and it shouldn't be to the extent where you can harm him.

* * *

The 100/10 rule

Never waste your 100% for that 10%.

Just to know you have been pouring into a leaking bucket.

This will raise a question over our own self-worth.

Continuously investing in non-reciprocating relationships and matters.

✹ ✹ ✹

Be aware of your destruction

When people around you realize that you are far more powerful and skilled, they will start destroying you. They would never want you to flourish. They would always make sure that you die in the state you are and not in the state you deserve.

Rarely you will get someone to push you forward to progress.

So, stop being stupid.

They knew exactly what they were doing and they knew exactly how much it would be hurting you.

Don't give them another chance.

* * *

No matter....

Whatever good you do to people; they will only remember your mistakes.

However nice and respectful you are, some people will still talk bad about you behind your back.

These most difficult times would make you more mature and stronger.

So, the friend who is your friend will always be on the side you have left

✻ ✻ ✻

_earn to

Hold on...

Let go....

Good people give you happiness, bad people give you experience

Worst people give you a lesson.

Beautiful people give us memories.

Some unexpected ones make us cry for things.

Some are with us just for our smiles.

Some unexpected ones love us.

Some trusted ones let us down unexpectedly.

So, never blame.

Out of the whole lot of people, we just need to know which hands to shake and let go & which ones to hold.

* * *

Never befriend people who put you in a situation that threaten
your own

Self-respect, peace of mind and values.

No response is also a response.

Because they wanted to, they did.

Your goals, your values and your heart are not common.

You are all the way, 'unique'

✳ ✳ ✳

A silence that speaks.

Whenever we come across some deceit or some sorrows due to friends around. We usually try to respond. We speak about it to others.

This will not let it go off.

Just be silent.

They will, sooner or later realize that you are silent because your silence is your response to whatever they did to you.

When devalued, discussion is not needed.

Silence is.

* * *

Not everyone deserves a seat at your table.

When you feel left out in a group of friends.

When you feel devalued amongst them.

Losing them might hurt but...

When you lose something bad, you actually gain something good.

Pay good attention to what kind of people are surrounding you.

You might be at the wrong table.

* * *

Don't consume the venom.

People who are utilizing your trust and money for themselves.

People who never stood by you in your sorrows and difficulties.

People who are with you but not for you.

Such people are venomous.

And such relations are venomous.

Keep your distance.

*** * ***

People are seriously funny.

If if you get fat, people think you eat much

If you lose weight, people think you are sick

If you dress well, people think you show off

If you dress simple, people think you are poor

If you are struggling, people think you are lazy

If you are successful, people think you are arrogant

If you are funny, people think you are immature...

People are funny, they keep saying even if you become God-like.

Ignore and just be aware of yourself.

✳ ✳ ✳

Draw your boundaries clear

It's never the third person who ruins your relationships, it's actually entertaining that third person.

Just know well those gossipers before they pollute your mind.

Keep them outside your boundary.

* * *

Abandoned ...?

People don't abandon people they love

People abandon people they were using.

The moment you become useless for them because you have attained the light, you are abandoned.

So, if you are abandoned, you were with the wrong people

✳ ✳ ✳

Not always to show...

Sometimes walking away becomes the best option.

Not to make them realize your value or anything else...

This is really very positive.

Because you have finally achieved the courage to respect yourself enough and realize you deserve better.

* * *

If you suddenly find yourself disconnected with your old friends thinking that they don't get you.

It's equally hard to make new friends because that connection is not there and so there is this version of old and new friends. This makes us feel alone.

But this is what life is doing for us.

Life is giving us the opportunity to grow in life and sometimes we need this loneliness for elevating in life and life is helping us to rebuild our life and our future.

Life is helping us to attract the right people.

So, keep fighting your way up.

Keep struggling.

✳ ✳ ✳

If somebody is happy without you, let them be.

Truth is always silent in nature.

These may be the people who don't deserve you or vice versa.

You can't change the minds of people who don't see anything wrong in what they are doing.

You can't always be okay with something they are okay with.

* * *

Awareness is the key

In all the different phases of our life, we rarely pay attention to our own sense of self awareness.

It comes to our mind when we are entrapped or stranded in certain situations by certain people, especially friends.

The way we observe people around us and the way people around us treat us is usually invisible till we start recognizing our disrespect.

The moment we come to know that we are actually being ignored and we are not actually of their utility, we sense our lack of self-awareness.

The best way to deal with people is to have the best sense of our own self-awareness.

The more we know ourselves, the easier it would be to know people around us.

❋ ❋ ❋

Faith & Patience

Things don't work out when, usually we want it to. The same thing applies to relationships and friendships as well. The moment we want someone to be there with us according to us, we create disturbances for our own mind. This creates expectations in our mind and we start losing both hope and faith.

Things work out slowly.

Slowly they come together.

Keep the faith & patience intact during the entire episode.

* * *

Time

Time is what life is made up of and life does to us what we do with our time. Taking good care of our time and investing it in the right thing is the key to having a little control over our life processes.

Love life by loving your time. Respect it, love it and you will see how time creates you.

In human lives and relations, time is a very prominent factor. We value the person who gives us time. We value the person who is there at the right time.

And several such things we come across.

Valuing everyone's time is of the utmost importance because time is time for all. My time cannot be more precious than anyone else's time and vice versa.

If the time with you is a little less, speed up with patience.

✹ ✹ ✹

Fit – Unfit

Never insist yourself to fit in where you don't actually belong. This will neither let you stay in your original version nor will it let you take a better version too.

So, always be in your own lane. It's always without the traffic.

Trust your way and move ahead with that trust. The lane would always render the character you own.

Attaining peace by dying is a hypothesis.

Living in peace is a bigger challenge.

Accept it and learn to learn life.

✳ ✳ ✳

Reaction is not a must.

Reacting to something or someone is usually in everyone's card of behaviour. Reaction should be proactive and not reactive. Always remember that our reaction will define the future of our relations. Reaction should be substantial and not just superficial.

Reaction should bring about good changes in the situation we are reacting to and it should bring about the positive side of the entire scenario.

Reacting for the sake of reacting is useless. Reacting to change for the better is useful.

Time of reaction is very important. Time drafts our responses.

Every reaction should be given a good time before it is being given.

If nurtured with values and wisdom, reactions become elixir.

Most of the human relations suffer because of untimed and non-substantial reactions.

So, make it a point, react with substance.

* * *

Life is the only beauty that exists.

We have been bestowed with the best that we could have been bestowed with, "Life".

Valuing what we have in our life is as important as valuing what we want from our life. Life has everything that our small minds can think or create. And in my experience, I learnt this truth only when I understood the 'art of thanking'.

After all the efforts to make my life beautiful according to my eyes, I realised that it's the beauty itself that I am trying to beatify.

How beautiful is each one's life?

The ideas that honk in our minds try to recreate our lives. Ideas that we ourselves create and believe that we have created something very beautiful.

We fail to accept what life has for us and we thrive to create our own ornaments for life. The more we try to design our lives, the more critical it becomes.

Acceptance creates positivity and it strengthens our mindset too. Once we accept our life as it is, we start seeing things in a better way and we find it easy to see its beauty.

Unless we accept life as it is, we will not understand the very fact that it's not our life that needs beatification but our vision for our life.

We look at our life superficially whereas we should look at it qualitatively. And each life is totally different from the other. We all are different, our lives are different but one thing is absolutely common, the giver of our life.

The moment we understand the connection between our life and the nature of life, we start moving on the victorious path of life. No need to become a monk by looks, be the one from within.

Life is what we all want to be the best.

But the approach towards it makes it one.

✳ ✳ ✳